Horrendous Healing

A Journey through Grief to Forgiveness—A True Story

Jack Brant Jr.

ISBN 978-1-64468-602-7 (Paperback)
ISBN 978-1-64468-603-4 (Digital)

Covenant Books, Inc.
11661 Hwy 707
Murrells Inlet, SC 29576
www.covenantbooks.com

Prologue

This memoir provides insights into many of my memories and thoughts over the past twenty-five years. Long ago, I had a very innocent view of the world and never thought that evil could or would touch me! I was wrong.

Death is so final, even when you believe in God the Father, God the Son, God the Holy Spirit, salvation, heaven, hell, and the afterlife. The thought of never seeing a special loved one again here on earth can be daunting.

This is my journey through loss, grief, forgiveness, and the aftermath of it all—a historical retelling of how *God was there throughout all situations, even though I had my doubts.*

I wrote this book to hopefully encourage and let you know that there are many others who know what you are going through. You are not alone.

I have a special place in my heart for people who have or are going through the grief process. In this book, it is my intention to provide relatable information. It is in no way exhaustive or complete, simply a glimpse. Also, there is no shame in getting or needing professional help. I'm hoping that what I went through will help other people to identify, confront, and work through the confusing emotions that make up the grief process.

My aspiration is that you will read what happened to me and come away with a clearer understanding of your emotions. I felt compelled to write my life story and shed light on the process known as *grief.*

My true story focuses on what I went through during the grief process after the tragedy of my father's murder.

1

IN THE MIDST

Life wasn't about constant excitement as my dad, Jack, always wanted it to be—whether working or fishing or both. In the spring of 1995, my dad was having a difficult time finding work as an electrician in Southern California. This was nothing new. He had many times of unemployment throughout the years because he had a hard time holding a job. Sometimes he lost jobs at the hands of others, and there were also times where he would deliberately quit a job. The truth was he was never happy with anything or anyone because he really needed to work on what was going on internally, but he would not do that.

I know that he had a tremendously horrible upbringing and that he was not wanted by his natural parents. His barren aunt-in-law, his oldest brother's wife, did want him and raised him as her own.

Because the oldest brother was an alcoholic, my dad didn't want anything to do with alcohol. Instead, he chose to put all of his effort into work, any work, at any time. His restless pattern, though, was often one week at a job, and the next week or few weeks, he was somewhere else.

Everything changed on Monday, August 27, 1995, after my mom, Cynthia, called my dad to find out how he was doing and if he had deposited his paycheck. She couldn't reach him, so she called back and talked to his foreman.

He gave her news that shocked our family to the core. He told her, "I don't know where Jack is. He didn't show up on Friday for his paycheck and didn't show up for work today either."

My mom was disturbed and surprised. She called me and my younger brother, Jason, to fill us in. I was twenty-five at the time and astonished. I thought, *That doesn't sound right.* During my life, my dad never willingly missed work. What happened?

My mom was truly concerned and, at that moment, all of her past and present problems with my dad became a distant blur.

She immediately called my dad's coworker, Rick, in Northern California. Both men had worked at the Shell refinery in Martinez, California. From what I had heard through my mom, my dad was happy at his new job and was earning plenty of overtime. Soon after he started there, he agreed to share a room at the E-Z 8 Motel in Vallejo with his new friend, Rick, a fellow electrician who met my dad at the Union Hall on July 31, 1995. They got along splendidly because Rick was from Colorado, and so the two of them had that in common. They decided to share a room to help keep their expenses down.

My mom wanted to find out if Rick knew anything.

"No, I don't," he said, and then he told my mom the same story that the foreman had told her.

Her mind spun with overwhelming concern, so she called me again, and I told her to file a missing person's report, and after some thought, she agreed. Since my dad was missing in Northern California. She thought that would be the best place to file. Then someone in her widening circle of concerned friends suggested contacting the local police department. She went to the Fullerton Police Department and filed a missing person's report.

The police officer she spoke with said, "This report will be sent throughout the United States. Don't worry. I see these types of things all of the time. Your husband is probably just having a midlife crisis and does not want to do the family thing anymore. If he did up and leave and he gets another job, we will be able to track him through his paycheck."

I told my mom that it did not sound like dad. I knew that they were having marital problems, but my dad never ran away from work and the opportunity to make money. I told my mom that we needed to look at the facts. Something bad had to have happened.

As the days went by, I continued to stay in very close contact with my mom. I constantly asked her if she had received any word from my dad.

She answered, "No."

She called the foreman and Rick many times for any new information that they could share—none. My dad's paycheck was still sitting on the desk in the office at the construction site. My constant thought was, *This does not sound like my dad.* There was no way that he would not be picking up his check.

The foreman knew that Cynthia could really use the money, so he mailed the check to her, which was a huge blessing. A few weeks later, a bill came to her apartment for the van that my dad had bought. He had decided to trade in his Geo Metro and buy a new Ford E-150 Conversion Van on August 4, 1995. The van was black with gray stripes. My dad loved the Oakland Raiders, and from what I heard, he loved this new van. The interior was gray and fitted with two captains' chairs for the driver and a passenger. There was mid-row seating and a seat that converted into a bed in the far back.

My dad sent a picture of himself standing next to his van. His face was blank and he was wearing a cowboy hat and cowboy boots. We also received a picture of him wearing an orange jumpsuit and a white hard hat with "Jack" in big black letters as he stood in the dirt next to a large oil rig. He had a slight smile and looked good.

My mom called my dad's motel room periodically to see how he was doing and to try and talk with him. She also called on paydays to see if he had deposited his check into their joint account. I hated seeing her so stressed about my dad.

*****

I remember hearing from her on August 12, 1995, that he had decided to start camping out of his van. He was living in his van and spent the nights under a bridge in Crockett, California. He was a loaner and wanted to spend his evenings fishing by himself.

Fishing was a hobby that Dad did every chance that he got. It did not matter if it was a lake, ocean, canal, river, or stream as he loved them all. He wasn't the best at it, but he did love to try. Every once and a while, he would get lucky and bring home some fish, but most of the time, he went for the excitement and thrill of catching something.

As a kid, I remember him taking my brother, Jason, and me fishing at the canals in Florida. It was great. We used these long bamboo poles with a string and cork at the end and dropped them into the water from a bridge. Dad usually brought up a snapping turtle and had to use a pair of pliers to get the hook out of its mouth.

In Colorado, I remember fishing at Cherry Creek Reservoir in Colorado with Dad and Jason. I was reeling in my line when all of a sudden, I had something on the other end. I reeled like crazy, and Dad said, "Bring it in." I had snagged a bass by the side of its gill. No kidding. Dad actually laughed. He couldn't believe I had caught the fish that way, and neither could I. Fishing was the one thing I could do with him that was, for the most part, a pleasant experience.

When I heard from Mom that he was going to spend more time fishing, I was not surprised. This was his retreat away from reality, away from society, where he could spend time by the peaceful sound of a river.

*****

As for the van bill, Mom was worried about whether or not to pay it. I told her not to pay. I figured it was Dad's purchase and he should be the one responsible for paying it. Mom said that she never signed any paperwork for the van and had no part in its purchase.

I continued to tell her, "You can't afford to pay that bill."

In September 1995, she received a bill from Sears and called me. The statement showed the purchase of a woman's engagement ring.

My mom's mind immediately jumped to *He's cheating on me!*

I said, "Mom, there's something wrong." I knew my dad was not the greatest guy in the world, but he was not a cheater.

"How do you explain the purchase of this ring?" she asked.

"I don't know."

I thought, *There's something wrong with this whole scenario, and I think there's been foul play involved.*

Mom wanted to know what had happened and called the Fullerton Police Department to disclose this new information to them. The department decided to assign a detective to the case who told her that Dad had probably left her for another woman. She was hurt to the core, and I tried to refute the detective's statement, but something was different and disconcerting.

Throughout this time of wondering what had happened to him, we continued to share the situation with family, friends, and people at church. We also continued to pray that God would deliver us from this misery and that He would allow us to know what happened to Dad. I often thought, *I wonder what he did this time.* It was a very difficult time. I knew my family was filled with anxiety and running out of patience.

In the middle of September, the finance company that held the loan on Dad's van started calling my mom. According to her, "They were like dogs on a bone." They started hounding her for money to pay the monthly payments. Even though it was difficult for her, she stood up for herself and told them that she could not make the payments and that she was not the one who had purchased the van.

The finance company representative was relentless and wanted to know where the van was.

My mom lost her cool and said, "So would I. Let me know if you find it so that I can have a word with Jack Brant too."

Calls kept pouring in at her apartment and at her place of employment. I felt so bad for her. I wished that she did not have to go through this harassment. Yet, we still had no knowledge about Dad. I had a bad feeling in the pit of my stomach that he wasn't alive, but I did not want to tell my mom that too many times.

About the third week of October, the finance company assigned a private investigator to the case. His job was to try and locate the van. He called Cynthia several times to see if she was covering for Dad, but he could tell that she wasn't, and then he offered to help. He had checked her phone records before contacting her. He saw that she had not spoken with Dad.

The private investigator told Mom that he had been assigned to the case for a while before he got in touch with her. He then said that he would gladly help her and share his information with her if she would share any of her information that she received from the detectives working the missing person's case. She was thankful for this solution and agreed to help.

2

THE FINDING

According to the detective's notes and what I've read and remember, the search for the body took a lot longer than the finding of the truth.

A young couple, Greg and Linda Woods, decided to hike in the nearby mountains with their two German Shepherds. They loaded up their old red-and-white VW van with their two dogs. One was a puppy named Carolina, and the other was a three-year-old named Sherman.

They traveled up the paved road for about a mile or so until it ended. Then they continued onto the dirt road that was riddled with trash and potholes. The mountain was frequented by local motorcycle gangs and partygoers who wanted to party and create chaos. This was not a place to be after dark, according to what the detective told me.

As Greg and Linda drove along the dirt road, they came to a point beyond the VW van's capability. They all left the van and started to walk into the unknown.

The dogs, which weren't restrained, took off to scout their new environment and were sniffing here and there. They were looking for a suitable spot to do their business. At the same time, Greg and Linda were making their way up the mountain. Greg reached behind his back and pulled out his new toy. Linda saw the BB gun but was not happy or impressed.

"Put that thing away," she said, but Greg decided to pop off a few shots. He shot several times at a nearby rock until he heard a ricochet that came whizzing back toward him. Then he started shooting at a beer bottle to see if the BB gun had enough power to break the glass.

Linda was walking past the bottle when it broke. She wasn't happy. She snapped at Greg, and they argued for a few moments.

Greg decided at that moment to put the gun away. His pleasure was not worth her wrath.

Meanwhile, the dogs were roaming the mountainside and were out of sight. Greg whistled, but only Sherman ran back. He was carrying a ratty, used, and weathered tennis ball that he had found. He dropped the ball by Greg's feet and waited for him to throw it. Greg picked up the nasty ball and threw it as far as he could. Sherman retrieved the ball after it had bounced a few times and returned it again to Greg.

The couple continued to walk to the top of the mountain until they came to a fork in the road. They decided to veer to the left. Greg whistled to grab Carolina's attention, but she did not respond as she was too preoccupied with her own ramblings.

After walking down this road, they saw Carolina's tail wagging as she stood on a down-sloping hill. The couple called for her to come, but she refused to obey. Greg was impatient and yanked her by the collar.

At that same moment, Greg realized that he had more to worry about than Carolina's obedience. Greg called Linda to come over to him. His concern was clear. He asked her to stay on the dirt road away from where he was. Linda actually waited. She sensed the urgency in his voice and held Carolina.

Greg was standing near a red sleeping bag with something in it. While looking at it, he grabbed a stick and peeled back the top layer. The horrendous smell overwhelmed his senses.

As he continued to open the bag, he realized that there was a rotting body inside. He felt queasy. By chance, he looked at his watch—2:35 in the afternoon.

Linda kept asking him if he was sure that he had found a dead body.

Greg said repeatedly, "Yes." He was gripped by adrenaline and terror.

They ran to the van with the dogs and drove to the local police station; it was a satellite station with no one there to help. They kept pushing the after-hours doorbell, but no one answered.

The couple knew that they had to get help, so they drove for another hour to the Sonoma County Sheriff's Department. There, they frantically approached the front desk and said they needed help immediately.

Detectives Steve Williams and Frank Morgan called the couple into their office and began questioning them about what they had found. Most of the questions were directed at Greg since he alone saw the body. The couple explained that they went to the mountain for a walk and they kept calling their dog, Carolina, but she would not come to them. The puppy was actually the one who discovered the body.

The detectives loaded up their equipment and assembled a team to investigate the couple's findings. Greg and Linda rode in the Blazer with Detectives Williams and Morgan.

A CSI crew was dispatched at the same time to meet them at the site. The day was quickly fading to night, and the couple was exhausted, but they knew if the situation were reversed that they would want someone to help them.

They pressed on. Upon arriving at the site, they got out of the Sheriff Department's Blazer as the sun was setting. Almost immediately, the detectives knew that it was going to be a long night of processing this crime scene.

The sheriff's crew unhooked its trailers and started the generators that supplied electricity for the overhead lights. CSI and the homicide detectives surrounded the sleeping bag and the nearby areas.

Williams grabbed one of the officers and directed him to get contact information for the couple and to take them back to the station to get their dogs and vehicle. Meanwhile, the CSI team took photographs and other evidence from the scene.

Williams and Morgan paid particular attention to the body and the bullet wounds. They searched the area for bullet casings but failed to find any. They noticed that the body had four bullet holes in the chest and upper torso—one was enough to kill.

3

UNIDENTIFIED

As the long night drew to a close and the sun rose on a new day, the detectives headed back to the station. Steve Williams went to the basement and met Jesse Gordon, the coroner, and questioned him about the body. Jesse was having a difficult time trying to determine if the badly decomposed body was a male or a female. He also concluded that the victim died of four shots at point-blank range, the victim never knowing what happened.

My mother and I didn't know what had happened either. I remember reading the police report and finding out that the Sonoma County Sheriff's Department had released the news to the local Northern California news stations.

The first one was on October 8, 1995, then another on October 20, followed by one on December 8, and a final one on January 19, 1996. These televised press releases generally started with the newscaster saying, "In the news tonight, the Sonoma County Sheriff's Department needs your help with a deceased body that was found near an area known as 'Motorcycle Mountain' not far from Guerneville."

Each press release had a more urgent plea for the public to help with any information. On October 20, 1995, the release mentioned that the victim's race, gender, and age were still unknown. What was known was that the victim was approximately 5'5" to 5'6" tall, had a slender to medium build, and was wearing a V-neck T-shirt and blue jeans. The jeans were approximately a 33"-inch waist and 27"-inch length. The victim had a full bridge of upper false teeth and a healed fracture on the lower left leg.

All of these press releases asked for the public's assistance and, if anyone had information, they were encouraged to contact the Violent Crimes Division of the Sonoma County Sheriff's Department.

On December 7, 1995, I remember being in my American History class. It was close to lunchtime. My mind continued to wander, and most of my thoughts were geared toward my dad or possibly what to eat for lunch. My teacher was an older lady, almost elderly.

She spoke monotoned, and I could not focus on what she was saying. Her words mimicked a Charles Schultz cartoon in my mind. It was like "Wah, wah, wah."

As I sat there, I was so zoned out that I barely even noticed a man had entered the classroom. Then I saw the teacher pointing toward me and the man starting to walk in my direction. As he got closer, I realized that he was John from the financial aid office. I thought there might be something wrong with my paperwork.

John said, "Someone is waiting for you outside in the quad area."

My stomach sank as deep down I knew what was happening, but my mind would not fully go there. I thought to myself that my suspicions were going to be confirmed by receiving the worst news of my life.

As I walked with John down the stairs and outside of the building, I saw my mother and brother. They did not have to say a word as I could read everything on their faces and in their eyes.

The coroner had confirmed that my dad had gone from missing to dead. It was so hard to hear about him being deceased.

I thought back to 1987 and remembered another awful time when my family decided to leave Colorado, a state that I loved. My dad once again had the desire to move to what he thought would be the promised land, the Golden State.

My mom was driving a brand-new Buick Century, my dad was driving a U-Haul truck, and I was driving my 1974 Datsun pickup. We had a tough go of it. When we were about an hour or so away from Las Vegas, my mom's Buick broke down. We had absolutely no idea why the car was giving us problems, but it was. It was July, and the midday desert sun was beating down on us. It felt like the sun had no mercy.

We sat there in the car, trying to figure out what to do. My dad thought it was a fuel problem. The car ran well when it was cold outside, but when it got hot, the car would shut off. My dad thought it was vapor-locked. He was good with cars, but this one had a lot of technology for that time period, most of which he was not familiar with.

He decided to drive my truck into the next town to see if he could find a parts store. Before he left, a man pulled over and offered his assistance and even gave us some money toward fixing the car. We refused his money, but he insisted. While talking to the nice gentleman, we learned that he was a Seventh-day Adventist. Unfortunately, he could not help with our car problem.

My dad took the truck and left while we sat there, trying to avoid the sweltering heat. There were a few drinks in the cooler that we had packed before we left the motel. Most of the ice had melted, but the drinks were still cool and provided some relief from the heat of the day.

About three or four hours later, my dad returned with some kind of universal fuel pump. It was late into the evening when we finally rolled into a small town with a Pep Boys. My dad had to limp that car the last few miles.

We ended up spending the night there. The next morning, the local Manny, Moe, and Jack could not figure out what was wrong with the car. The shop replaced the fuel pump relay and sent us on our way. At that point, we opted to drive late at night or early in the morning to avoid the heat as much as possible.

I have to say that upon entering California, I was excited about seeing the Pacific Ocean, but it had to wait. We arrived super late at night and had no clue where the beach was located. Those were the days before GPS.

Our first goal was to secure housing; however, my parents were ill-equipped financially for what it would take to live in California.

We could not even afford to rent a simple one-bedroom apartment. The cost of housing and the amount of money needed to move into a place was staggering, especially coming from the Midwest.

We kept hearing the same thing over and over again. We needed to have the first month's rent, the last month's rent, and a huge security deposit. We ended up staying in motels that allowed extended stays. Those were expensive too.

The motels usually had a small kitchenette and a small separation between the beds. My brother and I shared one area while my mom and dad shared the other. It was less than ideal and less than what we had in Colorado, but my dad had forced this move on us, and we were stuck.

I remember wanting to go back to Colorado as I never really wanted to leave. Being fresh out of high school, I did not make enough money to support myself. I was only seventeen years old at the time. I tried to make the best out of the situation and found work at the local Burger King. I tried to help our family out with what little money I made. I just held back a bit of an allowance to be able to go to a movie or bowling once a week with a friend from work.

The job that my dad was promised—the one we moved for— did not pan out. In addition to our difficult circumstances, he was now unemployed. He was left with no other alternative but to call Ethel, his mom. She sent out a bit of money to help us, but the car ended up getting repossessed. Not a big loss since it was a piece of junk.

My parents borrowed my truck for all of their errands or for my dad to find work. It took some time, but my dad was a very driven and determined man. He pounded the pavement and went through the yellow pages, calling every electrical contractor he could find to ask if they were hiring and to set up interviews. He finally landed a job with the union and saved up enough money to rent a two-bedroom apartment in Buena Park. It was a slightly rough area, not as nice as what we were used to, but it was for sure better than living in a motel or on the street.

I worked for a couple of fast-food joints, but I wanted something more out of life. I was not content with minimum wage. I ended up going to work for Winston Tire and then Mark C. Bloome Goodyear. I was a tire installer, and it was hard work. I felt comfortable working in the automotive sector and ended up going to work for an auto parts store as a delivery driver in 1989. It was there that I had the best bosses that I could ever have. I delivered parts to automotive shops around town, a specialty service, and I liked meeting the customers.

After a few years of working there, I accidentally crashed a delivery truck. I thought that I was going to get fired when the owner pulled me into his office. However, I was given a promotion to parts counterman, which meant that I would look up the parts for the customers and handle their money. I was happy. I now only had to deliver parts when the company was shorthanded.

After I proved myself at this position, I was given the responsibility to go out to different garages and do outside sales. However, I knew that this position would not allow me to support a family of my own. At this point, I had finished high school seven years ago. My friends encouraged me to attend college, but I wasn't real keen on the idea. I figured that it would be like high school, and I really disliked that whole experience. If I'm being honest, I did not like middle school either. However, I also thought and prayed over the idea of attending college. I decided to take a chance, and the doors opened for me to go.

That was me then, and this was him then: my dad was an electrician by trade, and he had bouts of time where he could not find work. This problem was sometimes solved in a day, week, month, or even longer. When it lasted too long, our family would go to our church and ask for help. I found it humiliating as a kid. I hated being poor. I hated that our family had to ask for help, but my parents did what they needed to do to survive.

My mom was the leader of the family. She made sure my brother and I grew up right and attended church every week in spite of what we might have wanted. I often tried to put up a fight against her, but it was useless. She always won. She always made the punishment worse than the task.

I remember thinking a lot about life and how I could make the finances better for my parents. We lived in a middle-income house, but somehow, we were always struggling. It was a major part of our lives.

We used creativity to solve life's problems instead of buying what was manufactured for a specific purpose. If snow boots were needed, this need was not met with money and a trip to a store. The solution was to find plastic bags and place them over my feet. Then the next step was to hurry up and put a pair of tennis shoes or rubber rain boots on. This way, I had a chance of keeping my feet warm and dry. I always wanted a pair of moon boots for the snow. The answer from my mom was generally, "We can't afford those, plus your feet are growing too fast."

Of course, there were times in high school that I was able to get a pair. They were usually two sizes too big, just so that I could grow into them. I loved moon boots. They were so squishy and felt like I was literally walking on the moon or what I imagined it would be like to walk on the moon. They were the best snow boots ever.

Meanwhile, on December 7, 1995, as I walked briskly toward my family, sorrow filled my heart. Tears eluded me for the moment. My mom, brother Jason, and I were still polite, and we thanked John for coming and getting me. I told my mom that I knew him from the financial aid office, but that was small talk. As soon as John headed toward his building and was out of earshot, she filled me in on the details.

The private detective had asked my mom to send my dad's dental records overnight to the coroner's office in Northern California. These records confirmed that the body in the morgue was indeed my dad. As if that was not bad enough, the body had been in the morgue since October as a John Doe case. As my mom continued to share the information, she cried. I wanted to cry, but I also wanted to find out as much as I could before I gave way to my emotions. I put my arms around her. Her pain was unspeakable. I tried to hide my emotions until I could deal with them in private. She then proceeded to tell us that two detectives were on their way to her apartment. They would be here in the morning to interrogate us and to make sure that we did not have any involvement.

Seems to me the mind goes backwards in a situation like this for the simple reason of wanting to know why anyone got in a situation like this. My parents were strapped for money. Back then, my dad was having a hard time finding work in Southern California. He was offered a job through the Union, but it meant that he would have to leave or move up to Northern California. My mom and I did not want him to "go up north." No one did, but he wanted it, and that was that.

My mom wanted him to stay in town because they were going through a rough patch in their marriage, and I wanted him to stay because I did not have a good feeling about his decision. I knew he was running away from his problems the way he always did. It seemed as though he was relying upon his own strength and not the Lord's.

No amount of begging and/or pleading was going to change his mind. He was set on packing up his stuff and leaving. This time, though, he was on his own. My mom refused to go on another one of his wild-goose chases. She decided to stay in Southern California. She had a lot of friends who she did not want to leave, plus she had a job as a bookkeeper for a local carpet company. My brother was on his own and working. My life was set, and I was living on my own with three other roommates.

I remember that my dad often caused my heart to ache. I loved him very much, but nothing was easy with him. He always said no to me as a kid. It did not matter what the question was. The answer was the same—"*No.*" So I used to avoid him and go straight to my mom. I knew that when she said no that she thought about the question first. One of the hardest things about my dad was that he would not listen to Godly counsel or any counsel for that matter. Once his mind was made up, it was very difficult to convince him otherwise.

His plan was to go up to Northern California and stay there for as long as he could to work and earn money. After he let me borrow his car one night for Bible study, he packed up. I was in utter misery over his decision. Every time I saw him, I expressed my concerns, and it was always the same answer: "I have to do this."

A few days before my brother's birthday, he packed up his white 1995 Geo Metro and loaded it with clothes, tools, and a sleeping bag and headed out. He promised to come back for my birthday, and I stayed in touch with him through my mom.

As the days grew closer to my birthday, my mom said he would not be able to make it back. To make matters worse, she told me that he had drained all of the money out of their checking account. Apparently, his windshield broke, and he had to get it fixed. I was disappointed. My heart sank. I think my mom was angrier about the situation than I was. My dad did come back for a few days on their anniversary in late July 1995. He came back to move my mom out of their apartment in Brea and into a lesser one in Fullerton.

My dad was fifty-three in 1995. He was a wiry man, about 5'7" and 140 pounds. Many people who saw us together did not believe that he was my real dad. He could never be accused of being lazy. He had so much energy and could never sit still. He was a workaholic. Very seldom did I ever see him enjoy a television show or just sit down and relax. I never saw him read a book. He was wired to work, and he loved it.

As a young man growing up, my father had plenty of strikes against him. He was the fourteenth child born in his family, and his parents did not want him. They were going to abort him. Ethel was as good of a mother as she could be, but his brother, Earl, who was acting like a father to him was not so kind. He was abusive and did everything he could to destroy my father's spirit and his life. My mom often shared stories of the mental and physical abuse my dad had suffered at the hands of his makeshift father/older brother. If my dad went to Earl for anything, his answer was always "No," even for simple provisions like food or clothes. He had to turn to Ethel, and they would secretly sneak off to get clothing. The abuse did not end there.

I can remember spending time as a kid at their farm in Somerset, Pennsylvania. It was never really much fun. It just wasn't the type of place I wanted to be. They were annoying. Plus, they had a cat, and I was deathly allergic to cats.

I quickly learned why my dad had turned out the way that he did. I always had a forgiving heart toward my dad, even though there were many times he acted like Earl toward me. I'm thankful that my dad never laid a hand on me, except for when he was spanking me for doing something wrong. He never hit me out of anger. He preferred to abuse me mentally by telling me that I would never amount to anything in life. He preferred to tell me that I was fat, dumb, and lazy. He preferred to be negative toward me almost all of his days. He preferred to shame me and break my spirit. He preferred to teach me that I had no real value as a person.

My mom, on the other hand, was my advocate. Sometimes, she would go to my dad and discuss matters with him in private. She had a way of getting my dad to try and come around on certain issues. She always provided me with the items that I needed. It got to the point where I never asked my dad for anything because I knew it was going to be an instant no. He was definitely a product of his upbringing.

Many pastors and counselors tried to help him throughout the years, but he was set in his ways. He would try for a while, but his lack of patience to see any real growth would always get the better of him. He wanted instant results for a life tormented by pain and suffering. There was only one time I actually saw him truly happy, and that was when he took a class for electronics.

My dad was an electrician and a good one. He was working on a job and got hurt. I think what happened was his partner said a certain power line was turned off when it wasn't. My dad was up on a ladder at the time and went flying off backwards after he made a connection. He ended up slipping a couple of discs in his lower back and was laid up at home for quite a while.

He was able to go to a trade school through workman's comp to become an electronic technician. He was so happy. He excelled at the program and was making diagnostic equipment and even received an award. As the training ended and he received his certificate, he thought that he would try to get a job using these newfound skills.

He quickly found out that the market was not willing to pay him as much as it did when he was an electrician. He was devastated and turned back to the world that he was all too familiar with—being an electrician.

*****

It was a summer day in Southern California, and the sun was shining bright. It was July 27, 1995, and I was on my way to my mom and dad's apartment to help him move their belongings into another apartment about five miles away. My heart was heavy as I met him. He was going back to Northern California. My mom was not successful in trying to talk him out of his decision to leave.

The marriage between my parents was strained, and only my mom was willing to put the work in to make it good. My dad was tired of being married and wanted to do things his own way.

I decided to just make the best of the situation by helping him move the furniture. Throughout the day, I continued to look up at the sky, and I really enjoyed the beauty that it provided. There were a few clouds scattered about, and the sky was a vibrant majestic blue.

My dad talked to me throughout the day, and he let me know that he was extremely proud of me. He even apologized to me for all of the mean and nasty things he had done to me throughout my childhood.

For me to hear my dad say that he was proud of me and that he really loved me meant more than I could ever express. It was able to correct a lifetime worth of hurt almost instantly.

As we continued to load up the U-Haul truck, my dad said he was so proud of how well I was doing in college. At that time, I was attending Fullerton College and was doing extremely well and getting fantastic grades. I was acing just about every class I was taking.

I had just gotten an old Toyota Celica from a guy at church, Don. He owned an automotive shop and wanted to help me out. It was $700, and he allowed me to make payments. My dad was even proud about the way I was trying to rebuild my life after all I had been through. My heart had never felt such joy as when my dad expressed his love, respect, and pride toward me. I thank God for that moment. I was beaming on the inside.

At lunchtime, we decided to take a break and went to Boston Market for rotisserie chicken with cornbread stuffing and a Caesar salad. We both shared concerns about the future. My ears still tingled and rang with joy at his words that he expressed toward me. I was also excited that there might be a great future once I finished school.

A couple of days later, my dad left twenty-seven years of marriage and headed up to Northern California. He was on his way to the Shell refinery in Martinez, California. I'd like to think that my dad's trip to Northern California was peaceful, but I do not know what was streaming through his mind. I know that the drive from Southern California to Northern California is filled with rolling green hills, pretty trees, and small towns scattered about.

He started working at the Shell refinery. I heard through my mom that he was happy. The company that he was working for had plenty of overtime, which allowed him to work as many hours as he desired.

At about that time, I remember hearing from my mom that my dad had decided to start camping out of his van. That was on August 12, 1995. He was living in his van under a bridge in Crockett, California. He wanted to spend his evenings by himself, fishing.

When I heard from my mom that my dad was going to spend more time fishing, I was not surprised. This was his retreat away from reality, away from society, where he could spend time by the peaceful sound of a river.

A couple of weeks into August 1995, I had started the new fall semester at Fullerton College, which was really close to my mom's apartment. I stopped by periodically during breaks in my schedule and made myself at home. As a college student, I tried to take advantage of receiving a free meal when and wherever possible. My mom was good about sharing. I wouldn't get homecooked, but there was always some kind of frozen something or other that I could pop into the microwave. My mom always had good drinks in the fridge and some sweet treats lying around. These good times quickly became bad times.

On December 7, 1995, we were told to be at my mom's apartment at 8:00 a.m. to discuss my dad's case with two Sonoma County detectives. My mom was hit the hardest with this information. As the two detectives arrived, I remember one of them, Steve, was short and stocky, while the other, Frank, was really tall and lurking. My mom had wanted us to be all together during the interrogation, but the detectives wanted to separate us. Both officers were polite but all business. The detectives split us up and talked to us individually.

Frank stayed in the living room with my mom. Steve took my younger brother out into the dining room. I had to wait in my mom's bedroom for my turn, which felt like an eternity. After about forty minutes, it was my turn, and my brother then had to wait in my mom's bedroom. Steve had a black notebook, and I tried to look at it without him noticing. He was on a mission, and so was I.

I wanted to find out what had happened to Dad. I tried to ask some prying questions to the detective, but he would not provide me with any information.

He then asked me about the last time I was in Northern California, and I said, "Never." That was the truth. I had never been to Northern California.

Steve then asked me if my dad liked expensive jewelry, and I said no. He asked me about the last time I talked to my dad, and I said the day we moved all of his belongings into this apartment.

As he kept firing questions at me, I kept trying to peek at the photographs he had in his notebook, but I did not see anything. We were probably useless to each other because he wasn't helping me, and I had no information to give him.

I did try to describe some of the personal effects that my dad might have had with him, but after that, they handed us their cards and said they would be in touch. I felt bad for my mom. Apparently, Frank was not very compassionate or sympathetic. Mom said he worked her over. My mom was upset and emotionally drained.

After the detectives left, we shared our experiences. I remember telling my mom that the detective had some photos, but I could not really make out what they were. She had tired eyes, and I could see this situation was really upsetting to her. This was an experience none of us wanted. After all, we had just found out the day before that my dad was dead—*murdered!*

The next press release was dated December 8, 1995. The news media released information that the victim had been identified as Jack Lee Brant, age fifty-three, of Fullerton, California. He was reported missing to the Fullerton Police Department on August 23, 1995.

> Mr. Brant's vehicle was recently found in the Guerneville area, and detectives were able to establish a connection between the vehicle and the unidentified remains. The circumstances surrounding Mr. Brant's disappearance and death are currently under investigation by the Violent Crimes Unit of the Sonoma County Sheriff's Department.

Christmas 1995 was almost nonexistent, and the best one I remember was being a young kid in Rockville, Maryland, at a pivotal age during adolescence. I wanted to be outside, exploring and having fun.

One night, two kids were bothering and bullying another kid. I thought that I would go outside and even the odds or at least see what was going on. Nothing really transpired. The two boys were ganging up on the one and spouting insults to belittle him. They were challenging him to various strength contests to test him.

They bet him that he couldn't lift a manhole cover. I don't know how, but I actually tried and was able to lift it. The two instigators were amazed and ended up leaving the scene.

I, on the other hand, had made a new friend, Keith. He had a deep impact on my youth. We were inseparable. I found myself at his house more times than I can count, and he was often at mine. It wasn't long before his family started inviting me to their cabin in the Pennsylvania Mountains.

There were a lot of adventures and stories that came along with that invitation. I remember his family having three-wheel ATCs that

Keith and I rode year-round. Whether there was snow, dirt, or even some mud, rain, and gravel, we were riding. It was fantastic.

In the summertime, we would get adventurous and take the machines to the top of the mountain and watch the hawks soar. Their feathers, like fingers, pushed down on the air as they swirled along the wind streams while looking for their next meal.

In the wintertime, the lake froze over and granted us opportunities to get to the other side where there was an old abandoned cabin. Gunshots had ravaged the glass and the building was dilapidated. On one Christmas, my parents spoiled me, and I was thankful as I opened the first box—a new pair of tan corduroy pants. Then I opened the second box—another pair of rust-colored cords.

Okay, I thought, *so far it is just practical stuff.* Then I was told to open a specific box. As I started to shred the wrapping paper, the image on the box revealed an ice skate, but not just any ice skate—a pair of Bauer ice hockey skates. I could not believe it. I immediately put them on and laced them up. They were huge, but I did not care. They were mine and they were awesome.

Later, I put some paper in the end of the skates and wore two pairs of socks. It did not matter as there was no better feeling than to skate on a frozen lake with my best friend and play hockey. He had sticks and pucks, and we shoveled paths on the frozen lake to form goals. We also had to shovel the areas where we wanted to skate.

We had a fireplace by the lake to warm ourselves when we got cold or wanted to take a break. One time, I was wearing my big puffy winter coat and got too close to the heat. The fire was so hot that it melted and singed a good part of one sleeve of my jacket. I was so worried and upset that my jacket was no longer perfect and that my parents were going to punish me. It was a total accident, and there was no way to hide the damage. Thankfully, my parents were gracious and understood. They knew it was an accident.

That was then, but the Christmas of 1995 was almost too existent. Everything I saw and perceived was moving in slow motion. Life appeared to be normal for everyone, except for me and my family.

I remember walking through the quad at school and watching everyone laughing and carrying on. They were having a good time as they talked, smiled, and laughed. In contrast, I had a heart full of sorrow and loneliness. For me, life was moving at a snail's pace.

That year, my family tried to go through the motions at Christmas, but nothing was working. Even church seemed like a waste of time. Families gathered to celebrate as some had not seen others for a while. Some only came because of the holiday. As for me, I could not sing the traditional Christmas songs or focus on their messages. I was just there, taking up space in a pew.

Days later, on January 19, 1996, a press release was sent locally in Sonoma County:

> A vehicle belonging to Mr. Brant was located in the Guerneville area several weeks after the homicide. The finding of this vehicle has helped the Sheriff's Department. An investigation into the circumstances of this incident led to the identification of Mr. Brant's assailant. He was identified only as Fred XXXXX, age 34, of Guerneville. A no-bail homicide arrest warrant was issued on January 19, 1996, by the judge of the Sonoma County Municipal Court.

Fred, the suspect, was found to be in custody in Moscow, Idaho, on unrelated robbery charges and was then served with an arrest warrant. It was not known when he would be extradited to Sonoma County to face a homicide charge. However, all of the legalities changed when Fred decided to carry out his plan to come back to California on his own.

4

THE MEMORIAL SERVICE

I remember the day before the memorial service as the sky was an ominous dark gray and the day was devoid of hope. The streets rang out with ever-beating rain. The sunshine was cloaked in darkness as the rain pounded harder and harder. I went with my mom and brother into the Big Lots on the corner of State College Boulevard and Chapman Avenue in Fullerton. I don't recall why we met there, but we did. I do remember my mom crying out that she hoped that it would not be raining tomorrow.

The cars swooshed through the puddles, and people ran into the shops. The aroma of spring pollen was in the air. I was not well, breathing hard in the humidity. Sorrow made my heart heavier. The torrents of rain brought on torrential thoughts during the day about tomorrow.

My mom and my brother fared no better. Hopelessness raised questions asked only of God: *Where do we go from here? How will we survive such a calamity? What's to become of us? If this happened, then what's to keep it from happening to me or all of us?* These answers were unknown and perhaps unknowable. The hope that had propelled me forward had stalled.

The next day, we gathered at the First Evangelical Free Church of Fullerton for the music, messages, and food. A well-known and respected pastor with the initials J. C. agreed to do the ceremony, and my family was pleased.

We were briefed about the ceremony. My friend, Aimee, sang "Amazing Grace," and the pastor recounted some of the times my dad had gone to him for help. Then my brother spoke, and I, lost in the fog of being lost, I don't recall what was said. I had eyes to see, but they did not see. I had ears to hear, but they could not hear.

5

GOING TO THE SITE

My mom and I drove to Sonoma County in Northern California before all of the legal proceedings took place. Under any other circumstances, this would have been an enjoyable road trip, but we were both too nervous about meeting with the detectives and the district attorney.

During the ride, we asked each other questions and tried to calm down. We somehow had some lighthearted banter. I really wished that my brother had come with us. He was invited and encouraged strongly, but he had to work and could not get the time off.

After the road trip and getting our motel room, we met and talked to the district attorney. We then went with Detective Steve Williams to see where my dad was found. During the ride, he talked to us about the case and the police report and told us all that he could.

I remember asking Steve a lot of questions as we went to the site. He was cordial and tried to answer the questions that he had answers to.

He drove us to the site, and I remember a point where we stopped on the dirt road and he said, "Excuse me," and reached into the glove compartment and pulled out a semiautomatic handgun.

He said, "We aren't going to the next spot unarmed."

We walked down a rough dirt road and saw where my dad was found. Without lingering, we returned to Steve's car and he drove us back to the station.

Back at the office, there was a long table where my mom and I sat while Steve got something out of his personal office—a big manila envelope. Inside were some of my dad's personal belongings that Steve spread out on the table. I don't recall all of the items, but I remember Steve told me that I could keep the watch and the flashlight. He then offered to help us in whatever way that he could.

That night in the hotel room, my mom and I tried to debrief each other about the day's events, and then we started fishing through the police report. I remember reading that the detectives had interviewed an eyewitness: Jules.

Jules reported that her boyfriend, Fred, drove up to her house with a brand-new van. According to her, the van was a real eye-catcher with a two-tone paint job that was black and silver. It sparkled as the sun beamed against the paint. The van was not cheap as it was a decked-out conversion van with plush king and queen captain's chairs—almost like La-Z-Boy recliners. However, Jules was not impressed. She thought the van looked too much like a billboard for the Oakland Raiders.

Fred decided to take Jules and her two boys to Disneyland, which was an epic road trip from Sonoma County to Southern California. They loaded up the van and traveled down I-5 for a chance to meet Mickey and friends.

Not long after starting the road trip and somewhere near Gilroy, Jules decided to get her camera from her tweed purse. She thought, *Wouldn't it be nice to catch these moments as photographs?*

As Fred continued to drive, Jules started snapping photographs of Fred and her sons. He looked over and realized that she was taking pictures. He quickly became extremely angry and started throwing the photographs out the window. Enraged, he pulled over to the side of the road and exploded at Jules. He yelled at her and pulled out his .380 nickel-plated gun and pointed it at her. He told her not to take any more pictures of him. He grabbed all of the photographs, except the one tucked between the seat and Jules' thigh.

In the backseat, the boys were gripped with fear and kept pleading, "Don't hurt my mommy. Please, don't hurt my mommy."

Fred calmed down.

As they continued down the road, the younger son, Jake, decided to take a few pictures. He reached into his Levi's and took out a disposable 35-mm camera. He was sitting far back in the van and avoided detection as he clicked off a few pictures of Fred.

As the hours and miles went by, the two young boys became bored and restless. They started playing tag and slapped each other and then noticed a scratched-up hard hat with a name on it. Neither boy could get the lettering right to see whose name it was.

They held the hat up and asked their mommy about the name. The black lettering read "Jack." Jules decided to ask Fred whose hat this was.

He responded, "Belongs to my friend I bought the van from."

As he pulled the van into a gas station to refuel, Jules decided to do a little more snooping. She opened the rear doors of the van and found a black nylon suitcase. She opened it and found a couple of collared dress shirts, pleated pants, and three pairs of Wrangler blue jeans.

Feeling safe because she was in a public place, she decided to ask Fred about the suitcase and clothes.

He said, "They belong to Jack."

She left it at that.

After the camera incident, she was afraid to push him too far. She did not want to see Fred get angry again as she needed to protect her two sons.

On reflection, I realized that *he was just down the street from us at Disneyland*. We did not know about his intention to take a vacation at Disneyland. Now he was *just down the street from us*.

After I read this in the police report, I felt very threatened and afraid, despite Fred being behind bars and on borrowed time for murder.

*****

Much of my life was spent moving. We went back and forth from Maryland to Florida, and then we headed to Colorado and eventually to California. I remember people asking if my dad was in the military. He was at one point when he was single. Now he was on a quest to find money and happiness by working hard.

We moved to Colorado in 1982, and he eventually took a job with the Colorado Highway Patrol as an electrician. *A great job,* I thought, but he was not happy there. He often complained about being bored and that there was little for him to do.

I thought, *So what? They give you a paycheck and health insurance.*

Life wasn't supposed to be about excitement as he always wanted it to be. He eventually quit and took a job with a local contractor. The truth was that he was never happy with anything or anyone because he really needed to work on what was going on internally, but he would not do that.

The church became a constant source of help and support for our family. Cherry Hills Community Church afforded me the opportunity to have friends and people to turn to. I loved my youth group. We were always going on camping trips, having BBQs, and weekly meetings where we would sing songs and learn more about Jesus. I didn't like being the scholarship kid, and I wasn't too fond of the main service. I always thought, *This is super-boring. Why would anyone want to listen to someone talk for over a half hour every week?* Maybe it was preparation for college.

It used to drive me crazy. I used to look up in the rafters and try to count the wood beams in the ceiling or see how many lights were hanging up there. I also always wondered why the church people dimmed the lights when the pastor prayed. Did the Holy Spirit only work in the dark? Were they trying to conserve energy in the 1980s?

In 1985, I started high school, and those were some of the worst years of my life. I hated them. I wanted to be left alone, and yet, people picked on me in my silence. I also thought it was super-boring and incredibly hard for me to pay attention.

I remember my parents and I meeting with my teachers and a counselor in the summer after my junior year. My parents asked what could be done for me to graduate. I wanted to drop out, and my grades were really low, abysmal. The teachers agreed that if I buckled down and did an honest year's worth of work, they would let me graduate. I had to turn everything in and not skip any of my classes. I also needed to pass each class with a C or better. I agreed. I knew that it was ultra-important to my mom and dad (especially my mom). I buckled down, did what was required, and got out of there. I graduated high school. I remember it was by the skin of my teeth, and my reward was a trip with my youth group.

The group leader took the graduating seniors to Lake Powell and the Grand Canyon for a week. We camped, water-skied, boated, and had an absolute blast.

One of the nights in Page, Arizona, I went on a walk with some friends. As we walked along the gravel road, I remember sharing my future plans. I wanted to start my own business so that I could help my parents with their financial struggles, which weighed heavily upon my heart. I hated all of the fights and concerns about money when I was growing up.

*****

When my mom and I met with the District Attorney (DA), it wasn't a very long meeting. He wanted to find out where we stood with the idea of a plea bargain. I wasn't really for it, but I didn't have any control in the matter. I asked the DA why we couldn't go for murder in the first degree. I don't remember his exact answer, but the spirit of it was that first-degree murders were extremely hard to prove, and the evidence wasn't there to prove this was first-degree. We could never figure out how my dad and Fred crossed paths. The DA mentioned that we would probably be able to win a civil case because it would be easier to win and did not require quite as much evidence.

Fred, the inmate, did fall under the Three-Strike Rule in California, and that meant he would get a fifty-two-year sentence. Because he injured a deputy during his escape in Idaho, he would have to serve at least 75 percent of that sentence.

In short, the inmate/prisoner would be about seventy-two-years old before he would be eligible for parole. My mom seemed fine with this, while I was harboring a lot of feelings and said, "If that is the best you can do, I guess we will have to accept it." I wasn't a big fan of the DA with his posh office and clothes. He had fancy degrees on the wall. I had no patience for him or the inmate/prisoner/criminal in this case. My mom handled everything with a much more impressive Christian attitude than I did. I was angry and wanted the inmate/prisoner/criminal to feel as much pain as I felt, but God had other plans.

6

SCATTERING THE ASHES

The day finally came when my mom was willing to part with my dad's ashes, and she made preparations to pour them into the ocean. She kept in close contact with my brother and me regarding her decisions, and then she received the appropriate permit from the Neptune Society. With all of the formalities done, she rented a nice boat for us, and I remember that trip quite well.

We all met at my mom's apartment in Fullerton, and my brother drove us all to Balboa Island. It was a beautiful day, the sky blue, and the weather pleasant.

We walked to the boat rental office to get everything in order. The boat was a tri-hull, and we boarded it and went out to sea. I have been on many boats before, both big and small, and I have never had a problem with seasickness, but this time I felt nauseous.

Out in the vast sea, my brother and mom became reluctant to part with the ashes, so as soon as I thought we had gone far enough, I took the lead and started pouring the ashes from the back of the boat.

It was weird to think that those ashes were all that remained of the physical structure of my dad's body. As they hit the ocean, the moment was surreal, like an unexplained life was being freed. My dad loved the water, and so it was appropriate that his ashes were spread at sea.

I handed the urn to my brother, and he poured more of my dad's ashes into the ocean. I sat in the back of the boat, and there seemed to be a sort of ongoing energy. I was expecting the dust to just scatter in the water, but it was a heavenly white substance, a cloud that ebbed back and forth in tune with the ocean's rhythm.

My mom poured out the remainder of the ashes.

The whole time we were on that boat, I kept fighting against being sick. We all cried at the permanence of the final statement that we had made about Dad.

Since we had the boat for a while, we cruised around and spotted sea lions sitting on top of a buoy. There was a humongous male and four females. That big buoy rocked back and forth with the waves, and we all just sat peacefully in the boat. We all knew that Dad would have appreciated being set free in the ocean. Death is so final, even when you believe in God, salvation, heaven, hell, and the afterlife. The thought of never seeing a special loved one again here on earth can be daunting. I know my dad wasn't perfect, but he was loved. I loved him.

To think of a loved one's last minute on earth is to wonder, did he or she suffer? Did they feel any pain? I wondered what Dad's final thoughts were. I hoped that he did not suffer for long, but I wonder what was going through his mind as he sat there in his van, being shot to death. I know it does not do any good to wonder about such things. His suffering was over in this life.

The sheriff's deputies seemed to think that his pain was ended quickly because he was shot four times point blank in the chest, torso, and neck. They conveyed to me several times that he never knew what happened. That was still no way for a man to die. He was alone and went down a path that eventually cost him everything.

7

PREPARATION FOR FORGIVENESS

I was attending CrossPoint Church in Chino, California, where I was also in a small Bible study with a group of men. Brian, who was the associate pastor, mentioned to me that he was looking for someone to get involved with the prison ministry.

At the time, I was rambunctious and ambitious. I was willing to do just about anything that I could to serve the Lord, so I volunteered. I thought this would be interesting, especially since I was coming from the opposite side of the spectrum, but I went with it anyway.

I was paired up with a slightly older black pastor from a different church. His name was Red and he was so upbeat, talkative, and excited to bring glory to God. I, on the other hand, was quiet, reserved, and not very vocal. One might say that I was a little more conservative as I was locked into my own mind and thoughts. I was checking things out, analyzing, and constantly evaluating situations.

First off, I met with the chaplain of the prison who was close to retiring. I thought he was a few years past due. He asked me about my background, why I was doing this, and so forth. I explained my story to him, about which he said, "Have you ever shared your forgiveness with the man who murdered your dad?"

No. I had forgiven the man who murdered my dad, but I didn't really want to make contact with him.

A man named Howard was a big black man with a heart of gold. He was high up in this particular prison and he was so excited to have me share my story.

I remember the first time that I went into the prison with Red to put on a church service. I was so nervous. It honestly scared me. Red and I prayed hard for what was about to take place. We left all of our personal belongings outside in our cars. We only had our driver's licenses to get into the prison. We left our world outside and entered one of which I knew nothing about. Red was aware of what was about to take place.

After going through sign-ins and different security gates, the experience became all too real. The only thing we had was a special pager (that looked like a garage door opener), a Bible, and Jesus— but it was enough.

After making our way in, we met with James, a porter, who was a prisoner with special privileges because he had good behavior and was a low threat to the volunteers. He had our backs, so to speak. He liked me. I really did not want to know what any of these guys had done wrong that ended up with them being in prison. I figured if I knew, it might give me a reason not to love them. However, the porter felt the need to share with me that he had been sentenced for armed robbery. He showed me his scars of where he had been shot in the side of his belly with a shotgun. It woke me up that this was no joke. This was real life. This was what happened when a person tried to rob an armored truck. He was a nice guy and was very protective of Red and me.

Though I didn't think we were ever in any real danger. Red had a garage-door-looking device with a button on it. I asked him what it was.

He said, "If something goes down, you or I can press it, and the deputies will come running in."

He thought it would take about three to four minutes for the deputies to get to us. That didn't sound too bad. Unfortunately, a lot can happen in that time frame. The good news was that the prisoners really liked us, the volunteers, the ones who gave of their time to visit with them. The chances of something bad happening to us were slim. I still could not help but feel a bit nervous. That's probably why I kept looking for something that I could use for protection.

As the church service got underway, I started to feel a little more comfortable with things. It was my first time in, so I didn't have a lot of responsibilities. I read one of the Psalms. I remember being impressed by the number of Scriptures some of these guys knew and had memorized. Here I was in seminary, and these guys could blow me away with the scriptures they could quote.

It was interesting, as the building was old, dank, smelled bad, had low technology, and probably a few more negatives, but I have never been to a more authentic church service where I felt the Spirit of God moving than when I was in that prison. Nothing has ever hit my heart harder in a church service than when a 6'5" man named James, who probably weighed 150-pounds and was dying of AIDS, requested that we sing "Nothing but the Blood of Jesus."

Those days in the prison were absolute blessings. Unfortunately, after a while, it got so hard to get inside the prison. It was almost like the devil knew what we were doing. I remember a couple of times right before we were going to check in that a fight broke out, and that meant the prison had to go on lockdown. I did get to share my testimony a few times there and even at church with follow-ups in front of a large congregation. I was asked to speak at the men's retreat. It was so awesome to be used by God and to bring Him glory.

So where did things go so sideways? I had different dreams and ambitions that got lost in the rubble of life. My life had not been a mere glimpse of steady happiness or success. In fact, for every success, there was often accompanying failures to contend with. There were bouts with depression, insecurities, and anxiety.

I remember wanting to quit the seminary. I was burned out, and it was a different way of viewing God, all academic and logical. I thought that it lacked heart or feelings. I love God, and this experience was all new to me. I used to only read the Bible, and now I had to use commentaries, novels, articles, and journals. I also had to read a lot of controversial views, which seemed like a waste of time and money. Why buy a book of an opposing view? It seemed like that was financially supporting the enemy. I enjoyed having a relationship where my feelings played a part too. The systems that I was learning seemed to beat that out of me. It felt like the legs of grace and mercy were being cut off at the knees as logic and scientific theories reigned supreme.

Maybe I'm not being fair and this was just my opinion or experience after all. I did have some great professors, one with whom I still keep in very close contact. He's a great friend, and I treasure our friendship. He has helped me out immensely. I was tired. I could not carry on, and I did not want to either. So I dropped out, gave up just one year away from graduating, but I did not care anymore.

I recalled that I almost did the same thing in high school and during my undergraduate studies. Next up and out, me in the master's degree program. I get about 90 percent there with my goals, and then I just want to throw in the towel or fall on the sword. In seminary, I really did throw in the towel. I wanted to get a job and join the professional crowd. I searched high and low. I interviewed and received calls back, but no one would hire me. I was so frustrated. I did everything possible to get a job, and yet the harder I tried, the more the doors slammed shut.

At that time, I was also losing my house. I tried to negotiate with the banks because I was financially devastated, but they would not negotiate. We were destined to lose our house. I kept wondering where God was in all of this. I knew it wasn't His fault the economy was in the tank. It wasn't His fault that the banks would not help or restructure our loans. It was not His fault that I could not get a suitable job to pay the bills.

My ego was crushed, having been raised to pay the bills first. While some people were living the high life, I was making sure we had something in the bank. Our vehicles were paid off. We had some bills, but that was normal. The banks seemed more content to take our house rather than to help. I called the banks, and they acted like I had never called or talked to them before.

I had to start from the beginning every time I called them. It was ridiculous. "Hello. Help me."

"Sorry, what's that?"

Help was a four-letter word that the banking system never intended to use. It did not matter that the US president had signed policies into place that were supposed to help the homeowners. The banking system disregarded them. I ended up being thankful that God allowed us to sell the house and get out of it gracefully.

I continued to pray about the situation, and the answer I kept getting was to go back to seminary. I finally gave in and reenlisted. I was fully restored. A certain professor came alongside of me, and we spent numerous amounts of time enjoying the outdoors on our mountain bikes. He saw life in a manner that I respected, and it made me want to be as dedicated as he was. His encouragement and support were, and still are, true blessings.

*****

I remember finally recognizing the power of the Holy Spirit while sitting in the bathtub one day with the shower pouring down over me. All of a sudden, it was as if a great divide took place internally. During this time, I saw my sins in their fullness. It was painful, and I bawled like a baby. My tears, sorrow, and crying were uncontrollable. I saw how wretched I truly was. There's no way to sugarcoat it. It was as if I saw the fullness of sin placed on me from Adam.

Each and every one of us is sinful: murderers, idolaters, thieves, adulterers, gossips, fornicators, and every other sin ever listed. You may never see this in its fullness, but we are. We may never have ever committed some of these sins, but they were put onto us by Adam and Eve. We may not see it because we are blinded by the god of this age or by our own ego.

The good news is that it can all be forgiven by the price that was paid by Jesus Christ. His blood and body wash us and make us clean. In the courtroom, the only thing that will keep us from a guilty verdict is the blood of Jesus Christ. Without it, we are guilty. He paid the cost for every man, woman, and child.

I know that after my spiritual eyes were opened, there was no way I would want to enter that courtroom and be found guilty. Thank you, Jesus, for setting me free from my sins.

I think this was another reason why I was able to reach out to the man who killed my dad. I figured that I was no better. The only differences between him and me were that I have Christ's blood applied to my account and I have never physically carried out murder. However, there have been times where dark thoughts and/or feelings have entered my heart and mind.

I remember being influenced gently at night as I tried to sleep. I was somewhere between a waking reality and sleep. The thoughts remained the same: *I needed to forgive the man who murdered my dad.* I conversed with myself, but the thoughts continued to be that I needed to let him know by writing him a letter that he was forgiven as far as I was concerned. I did not want to do this on my own accord. I thought that what I had done in the past was good enough. Yet, I kept getting nudged that I needed to forgive him in a tangible manner. I needed to write him a letter and let him know. I felt as though God wanted me out of the way and to fully release him into His hands.

After many interrupted nights and with the same message in my mind, I set forth to write a letter of forgiveness. This was one tall request. I prayed about it, my wife prayed about it, my family and friends prayed about it, and people at church and the grief group prayed about it. My mind was sharp and filled with scripture. I set up a mailbox at school to receive mail in case he did respond. I figured it would be hard for anything bad to happen to me at school where thousands of people attended. I did not know who or what I was dealing with, and I wanted to protect my family. I wanted to be smart about it.

I remember sitting upstairs in my office, a quaint little room. The computer was in front of me. I started to think, *What am I going to write? How do I word things? After all, this person murdered my dad in cold blood.*

I didn't want to be offensive, but I also needed to be truthful. I really believed that God inspired me to write the following letter, and I sent it on July 8, 2011.

Forgiveness Letter to a Murderer

To Whom It May Concern:

Well, let me start out by saying I don't know how much mail you receive, but I hope that you will read this letter in its entirety. I am sending you this letter because I am wondering how you are doing. You are probably unaware of who I am, but it will become quickly apparent as you read on.

I am the elder son of the man whose life you took in 1995. This letter is not an attempt to be mean or belittle or project any other type of negativity. It is a sincere attempt to let you know that I have forgiven you for the act that you committed.

I have spent a lot of time over the years being angry at you for taking my dad's life. But I have found that anger did not accomplish anything productive, though it took me many years to realize this fact.

After about six years, I realized that I needed to forgive you for what you did to my family by taking my dad's life. This was a process of continually laying down the anger, hurt, and resentment, but over time and by the power of God, those feelings subsided and eventually lost any type of control or hold upon my life.

I know that you are unaware of this because I have never disclosed this to you before this letter, nor have I ever had any communication, other than the nasty letter I wrote that was probably read to you during your sentencing.

You may not even care, but I felt it was important to share with you that I have forgiven you for taking my dad's life. I also wish to share the power of the Lord Jesus Christ with you.

One day a few years ago, the Holy Spirit revealed to me my own heart. It was not a pretty sight. I saw all of my sins, and my heart had been exposed and circumcised. It left me humbled, and the very core of my being was ever-present before my spiritual eyes. I, too, was a sinner and saw my need for a savior, which pointed me to the cross.

Though I had forgiven you with my new heart, I started to feel somewhat sorry for you, which led me to pray for you. Now it isn't an everyday occurrence, I must admit, but sometimes I pray for you and that you would see your need for Jesus Christ. Now I must confess that I believe everyone needs Jesus, and the thought of eternal separation from a loving God is just too mind-boggling for me.

If you were/are held in bondage or a slave to your own sins, I did not/do not want to be one of the ones who was/is hindering a mediation between you and Christ. Hence, this is another reason for this letter: I want to say that I have forgiven you for what you did to my dad, but what is even more powerful is that God in heaven is willing to forgive you if you choose to let him.

It is speculative for me to think you need forgiveness. Maybe throughout the years, you have come to a saving relationship with God through His Son Jesus Christ. I do not know. Nor do I know you. I just wanted you to know that whether or not you receive this letter, I have forgiven you for what you have done to my dad. I know that I will see him again when I pass from this life into eternity and I will join him in heaven.

In spite of his sins or my sins, the Apostle Paul assures me of this truth in Romans 10:13, where it says, "For whoever calls on the name of the LORD shall be saved." But this is not a generic god. The LORD is Jesus Christ who Paul makes clear in Romans 1:3–4 where he says, "concerning His Son Jesus Christ, our Lord, who was born of the seed of David according to the flesh, and declared to be the Son of God with power according to the Spirit of holiness, by the resurrection from the dead."

My true hope for you is that you will see your own need for God and that He will be the LORD of your life. If you have any questions, comments, or interest in writing to me, I receive my mail at…

The Murderer's Response

I wondered what the result would be after I sent the letter. Would he get it? Would he read it? And would he respond? I also wondered what would happen if he did respond.

Some of my questions were answered when I received this letter in my mailbox at school on August 29, 2011. I debated whether to read it or not.

Fred's Real Letter to Me

Mr. Brant:
I don't really know what to say in this letter and I must admit I was shocked and surprised to receive a letter from you. I knew immediately when I read the envelope who it was from "by the name." Apprehensively, I opened your letter. One

of the first things that you mentioned was that you hoped that I would read it in its entirety. I assure you that I have read and reread your letter many times over, along with sending a copy of it to my own family. I received your letter on the twelfth of July, and it has taken me this long just to be able to put this letter together, not because I'm so busy, more like trying to find the right words to say, if there is such a thing. I have never written a letter like this before, and I find it very hard to do. I don't imagine people do write letters like the one that you sent me or the one that I am writing now. I will just do the best I can.

I did not know that your father had kids because I didn't really know your father. You mentioned that you had written me years ago through the court system and that they were going to read the letter to me at my sentencing; they did not read any letters to me at my sentencing hearing

I'm sorry for what happened that night. Your father losing his life at my doing is what I mean. I have never come to grips with the whole thing and don't think that I ever will. The pain "for myself" does not come from being in prison; it comes from all the pain that I have caused to so many people. What I would like is for you to know that I'm truly sorry for all the pain that I have caused you and your family. I cannot even imagine what you must have gone through and still suffer to this day.

It must have taken you a lot of soul-searching and courage to sit down and compose that letter to me after all these years, and with that being said, I want to thank you for forgiving me, although I believe that it gives you more comfort than myself because I will never forgive myself for my actions. I relive that night all the time, and it is always on the forefront of my mind as I'm sure that it always will be.

You mentioned in your letter about having God in your life. Is that how you found the strength to write me? If things were reversed, I don't think that I could have done what you did. Your letter shocked me, and it has taken me some time to process it; like I said, I did not know that you existed. Now knowing that you are there and from your letter, I got it that you also have siblings just adding to my sorrow. I don't believe that adding to my sorrow was your intention or just maybe it was; I don't know because again, I don't know you. All that I do know is that I don't blame you for your hatred or anger toward me. I never found or had God in my life and most likely never will. I have seen people with God in their lives, and it seemed like they were happy, but it just never did anything like that for me.

This letter is not about me. It just that you, in your letter, brought it up, and I just thought that you wanted to know that for some reason.

I hope that I have expressed myself in the right manner because I'm not very good with expressing myself on paper; it was not my intention to upset you any more then I already have. Take care, and I will only write back to you if you find that you have questions for me that I can answer.

Thank you for taking the time to write me.

Sincerely,

X-XXXXXXX

*****

I did not know what to expect or what awaited me in his letter, but I had to read it. I remember reading it to the Grief Group the following week. It brought up emotions for me. I remember that I had to work through areas of grief that once again rose their ugly heads. I had a certain amount of anger and other emotions that I thought I was done with, but I wasn't. These areas no longer had the power or strength they once did, but they still needed to be dealt with. I continued to pray about them and to write about them. I decided to write another letter to the murderer after praying about it. The second letter I wrote was to address some of his questions and what I thought God wanted me to write. Here is the second letter from me to him that I sent on September 20, 2011.

Second Letter to a Murderer

> Wow, what can I say, except "thank you?" I received your letter. To be honest, I did not know what to expect, and I had kind of given up hope of receiving a response. Part of me was thinking, do I read this or not? As you will see, I read it, and I must commend you on your letter. It really meant a lot to me.
>
> In your letter, I sensed that you were really honest, sincere, and humble. I must admit that as I read your letter, my tears flowed, and it wasn't what I was expecting, but not in a bad way.
>
> You asked me if I was able to forgive you because of God, so I will address this question and say yes. I, in myself, find forgiveness very hard to do, but when I pray to Christ, I am able to forgive. Sometimes, I have to keep praying to forgive because I want to hold onto the wrong, but eventually, I release it.
>
> One day, I was reading a particular portion of the Bible, and I was convinced in my own conscience. I hope you don't mind me sharing this

with you. The context of it is when Jesus's disciples were asking Jesus how to pray. He responded by saying this is how one should pray in Matthew 6:9–13: "Our Father in heaven, Hallowed be Your name. Your kingdom come, Your will be done on earth as it is in heaven. Give us this day our daily bread. And forgive us our debts, as we forgive our debtors. And do not lead us into temptation, but deliver us from the evil one. For Yours is the kingdom and the power and the glory forever. Amen."

Yet most of the time, this is where everyone stops the prayer, but it goes on in verses 14 and 15 with what absolutely convicted me. "For if you forgive men their trespasses, your heavenly Father will also forgive you. But if you do not forgive men their trespasses, neither will your Father forgive your trespasses." That last part really stuck with me. I do not mean to get too preachy. I just thought you might want to know.

I know that you also mentioned that dreadful night has remained on your conscience or at the forefront of your mind. I am sorry to hear that. I do not bring this up to aggravate the situation. I do not take any delight in this; in fact, the reason I am writing is to let you know that you can be forgiven, but only if you are willing to be forgiven. I have forgiven you, and that still holds.

What I said in the other letter is still as true today as the first time you read it. As for your own peace of mind, unfortunately, that is between you and God. Jesus Christ is the only one who can truly forgive you and set you free. He has already done the work, which was to die upon the cross, resurrect, and ascend into heaven. All have sinned and fall short of the glory of God, and so each person needs to make a decision whether they are going to have faith and believe in that or not.

The Bible says, "He stands at the door and knocks and to whoever answers He will in no way turn away." I guess that I can't really get away from the preaching thing, so if you will bear with me for a couple of more sentences, I promise not to preach anymore unless you ask me more questions in the future.

There are people in the Bible who took the lives of others. Moses took the life of an Egyptian out of anger because he saw the Egyptian mistreating God's people. King David had a man murdered so that he might hide his adultery with Bathsheba and gain her as his wife. In the New Testament, there was Saul, who was converted to Christianity and his new name became Paul. Before Paul's conversion to Christianity, he persecuted Christians because he was a zealous Pharisee. He ended up being a great man of God and experienced Christ's forgiveness firsthand and to its fullness. He also wrote quite a bit of the New Testament as a changed man. If God can forgive these people, why can't He forgive you?

Again, I sincerely thank you for the letter that you wrote to me. It did mean a lot and it was quite unexpected. I do appreciate your honesty, sincerity, and humility. It must have taken a lot for you to write that letter. If you have any questions, comments, or interest in writing to me, I receive my mail at...

Second Letter from a Murderer

On October 1, 2011, I received another letter from him in my mailbox at school. Here is what he wrote.

> Hello, Jack,
>
> I hope that you don't mind me calling you by your first name. I still find it hard to believe that we are corresponding at any level because of the circumstances in which our lives have brought us in contact with one another. I say circumstances of life, and I'm sure that you would say that somehow God has made the connection, perhaps; I don't know. I must admit it would be wonderful if something good came out of this tragedy.
>
> Jack, I say tragedy because I still have trouble after all these years thinking of the words *murder* or *homicide*, so excuse me if I take some of the bite out of it, but I must say that it is a "tragedy" by definition.
>
> Maybe I should give you a little background on myself and my letter-writing ability. I'm not very good at it, and I find it hard to express myself on paper or in person as far as that goes. I guess what I am saying is that you will have to excuse me for whatever mistakes that you come across in my letters. I guess that just maybe I'm getting ahead of myself because this just might be the last time that I write to you because to tell you the truth, I don't have the foggiest idea what I'm doing writing to you at all.
>
> I mean, here it is Saturday, 6:00 a.m., and I woke up at 5:00 with the desire of writing back to you on my mind. No, I'm not a funny style. What I mean by saying that is I don't know what

I'm doing writing you because you started this correspondence.

Do you find it as intoxicating as I do? I don't mean that the wrong way. It's just kind of mind-boggling to me and the last thing I would ever have expected to be doing. Should I never write to you again or what? I'm confused on the right thing to do. Now that I'm putting even more thought into this writing to you thing, I think that I will just let you make that decision and get back to me with the answer before I send you any more letters, so please answer that question for me if you respond to this letter. If you don't, I will understand and not continue to write to you.

Jack, I was talking to my daughter the other day, and I told her about you and your letters, and she was very surprised that you had written to me. My daughter and ex-wife are very much Christians and have been on me lately about reading Romans, but I must admit I have not yet read any of it.

To tell you the truth, I don't even own a Bible and never have. I guess that I will have to pick one up and see just what you guys are trying to say to me. I guess that you just might have been getting the idea that I have not ever read the Bible, and that would be very true.

They (my ex-wife and kids) used to try to get me to go to church with them, but I did not want to. I went a couple of times, but that was about it. I just did not get it. The conversation that I had with them was just a couple of days ago, and while I was talking with them, they were both crying about how my life has turned out.

Yeah, seventeen years later, I'm still hurting people by what I have done. I don't think that it will ever end; at least, it does not seem so.

I must tell you, Jack, that I have told this story (our corresponding) to everyone that I come in contact with, and that means everything to me because I find it fascinating that you and I are writing at all; at least, it does to me. My brothers and sisters know every word that you wrote to me in that first letter. I hope that you don't mind that I shared that letter with them. They all wanted me to write back. That just might have been the hardest letter that I have ever written, and that is why it took me so long to get back to you.

You mentioned in your last letter that the letter I wrote to you was not what you expected. What did you expect? You also mentioned that you had the thought "Should I read this or not?" That is the exact feeling that I had about your first letter and, to tell you the truth, just a little bit on the last letter.

I was relieved to see that my letter was received and related to for the most part the way that I had meant it to be. I guess that I'm waiting for you to start yelling at me or saying some kind of hateful or hurtful words. I don't know. I just don't want any more negativity in my life. My life has been full of negativity the last seventeen years. Don't get me wrong as I would not blame you for those feelings or wanting to express them; but, Jack, there is really nothing that you could say to me to make me feel any worse then I already did before I found out that your dad had children of his own.

Just to change the tempo of this letter, I want you to know a little more about who I am just in case you wanted to know who you were writing to besides the guy who destroyed your family.

I'm fifty years old and I'm from Alaska all my life. I have three kids and an ex-wife as I have already told you. My son is twenty-eight, my oldest daughter is twenty-four, and my youngest daughter just turned twenty-two this month. I worked in the oil fields in Alaska most of my employed years. I went to Alabama for a short trip, and that is where I met my wife.

Now they all live in Winter Park, Florida. So I don't ever see them, and for years, we did not have contact, but that has changed in the last few months for some reason that I don't really understand, but I welcome it with open arms.

I also have two brothers and two sisters in Alaska. I'm the youngest of five. My mom passed away just about a year ago, and I never knew my dad. There is much more about my life, but most of it is not very nice on my part.

Jack, I am not the man that I use to be by any means. I did drugs for most of my adult life and hid it from most people. I do not know how I ended up with such a wonderful wife and beautiful life with them, but as all things at that time of my life, I destroyed them also and really went downhill from there.

I have been clean and sober since I have come to prison, and I cannot remember any time in my life that my thinking was any clearer than it is now at this point in my life. I could go on, but I don't want to just ramble on about me or how things used to be. I just hope that this letter does not reflect on me any other way then the way that I intend it to because I do not mean any kind of disrespect to you, and I hope that I did not offend you in any way.

I guess that I will close this letter with that thought. Oh, yeah, don't worry about being too "preachy" as you call it when you write to me, and thank you for your letters.

P.S. If you do write back, and if you don't mind, please tell me something about yourself so that I have a better idea who you are.

Sincerely,

X-XXXXXXX

I remember the second letter that I received raised more emotions for me. It seemed as though he was more intoxicated that I wrote to him than accepting responsibility for his actions or the gravity of the situation. I had a hard time with anger and forgiveness after the second letter I received from him. I think what was really upsetting was that he referred to that night as a tragedy. I agree that it was a tragedy, but he was responsible for that tragedy, and it was downright murder.

The only positives in the situation were that he capitalized the "G" for God and his daughter and ex-wife were devout Christians who had been trying to get him to read Romans.

He knew that he had destroyed my family. That is what the devil does. He comes to steal, kill, and destroy. That is his modus operandi.

I was really bothered and disturbed that he seemed to be missing the same sense of remorse that he had in his first letter. It was at this point that I decided to stop communicating with him. I had done what I set out to do, which was to extend my forgiveness, even though he never sought it. I did it to be obedient to God. Yet, I was dissatisfied with myself that I did not carry on further with the letter writing. I left things in a state of mediocrity, which felt unsettling to me, like I had failed to finish.

I'm not sure if Christ wanted me to continue or not. I prayed about it, but I did not receive an answer either way. Plus, if Fred wasn't going to accept responsibility, I really did not want to perpetuate more of a relationship. I felt like God wanted me to write the letters and to let him know that I forgave him. I could not have done any of this on my own strength. It was truly the power of the Holy Spirit within me that gave me the strength and helped me to continually lay my emotions down. My heart wanted to fight and hold onto the anger. Yet, my mind continued to lay it down.

He had worked in the oil fields all of his life. It took me many years to realize that this may very well be how my dad came into contact with him. We always wondered how it came to be: How did my dad meet Fred? How was Fred in the van with my dad? The oil fields might just be the way the two came into contact with one another.

After I received the second letter, I had severe panic attacks that stemmed from a horrible dream I had one night in which I was standing before God. He was so disappointed in me and sent me to the deepest parts of hell where it was complete and utter darkness.

As I was falling backward, the light grew darker and darker and more distant. It scared me more than words could ever express. I was so scared to die at this point. I even ended up in the hospital a couple of times and had to go to the doctor's office to seek treatment. They had to give me some shots to settle me down and to calm my nerves. My doctor ended up prescribing me some medicine to rid myself of the panic attacks. My mind kept telling me it was just a bad dream and Jesus had really saved me, but I could not control the emotional response I was having physically.

At the same time, a really good friend of mine that I had worked with at Isuzu had died. He was riding his motorcycle one morning and was ejected from his bike. The accident happened on Ortega Highway. He was the one who had also gotten me into motorcycles and whom I ended up buying my motorcycle from. We did so many rides together. We put thousands of miles on our motorcycles together. I witnessed to him several times, but I don't know if he ever became a believer or not. I hope that he did become a Christian.

Forgiveness of a Murderer

I became convinced that Jesus did not hold onto His rights. He forgave the people when He was being crucified. He asked the Father to forgive them, for they knew not what they were doing. In Matthew, we see in the Lord's Prayer that we are to forgive people of their sins that they commit against us, especially if we want our own sins forgiven. This convinced me. I always loved the Lord's Prayer but was unaware of verse 15. The Bible also teaches that anger is okay but not to give the devil an opportunity. I had spent a lot of time being angry. It was powerful. It was like a drug. It gave me strength. It kept me functioning or so I thought. I had some of the greatest workouts in the gym when I was angry. I had to let it go.

There came a point where God said, "Enough. Knock it off. You need to forgive the man who took your dad's life."

I would like to think that it was a one-time occurrence. However, I had to keep laying it down and handing it over to God. The darkness wanted to come back into my life. It took me a solid six years to forgive the man for what he had done, the dreams he had crushed, the anger he had caused, and to let go of the hold that the event had on me in general. Also, it was not an easy open and shut case. There were many things our family had to endure. We had to go through the missing of my dad. There was the escape of the inmate. There was the legal system and all of its woes. There were a lot of situations that delayed the grief process or put it on hold.

Delayed Grief

I faced many delays in dealing with my grief. The first time was when Fred, who murdered my dad, escaped from a maximum-security prison in Moscow, Idaho, and went to Disneyland in California for a week. However, it was a great thing that he did. God used that situation to keep him in California, which worked to my family's advantage. Idaho did not want to send him back to California, so when he went there on his own forced accord, it meant the State of California could keep him. After all, the murder charges were more important than armed robbery ones, but he did injure a deputy when he escaped from Idaho.

His escape definitely wreaked havoc on my family. We were so worried that he was coming to California to cause problems with the rest of my family. I remember being frightened that he was going to kill me or my brother or my mom. He was only ten minutes away from where we lived. It would have been very easy for him. It was so unnerving. This heightened our grief even more.

Our family's grieving was also put on hold as we went through all of the legal proceedings. We were in constant contact with the District Attorney of Sonoma County. We had to decide if we would accept a plea bargain or if we were going to go to court. Our decision was made a little easier because he fell under the three strikes and out policy. My family agreed to the plea bargain and knew that he would be an old man before he would even be eligible for parole.

Before my father died, I tried to help other people. Once the emotions rolled in, I realized that I had to work through the grief. It really changed me, and it was hard to get used to the new normal. Grief can make a person feel an array of emotions. I learned that family was much more important. Unfortunately, grief can tear families apart. Lord knows that if there was a magic pill or formula to escape the pain, I would have signed up for it instantly—but there isn't.

Grief holds a key to a door that must be walked through. There's no way to avoid it. It will knock and hound a person until it's dealt with. There's no escaping it. It's meant to change you.

One thing I really admired about the story of Job in the Old Testament was the end product of Job's life. He was super-obedient in the beginning. Satan was allowed to make Job's life miserable, which he did. At the end, though, Job had a genuine relationship with God. They conversed with each other. Sure, Job had his fortunes restored, and they exceeded in abundance, but what was really cool was the interaction between God and Job. There was a personal relationship, and Job was filled with the Majesty of God. Also, the relationship was more than duty, sacrifice, and/or service—it was deeply personal.

Dealing with Grief

Overwhelming feelings abounded, such as rage, anger, anxiety, restlessness, frustration with sorrow, sadness, depression, obsession, and a side order of sleeplessness just for good measure. These are just some of the feelings that accompanied the grief that I felt or dealt with throughout the years.

The horrible and terrifying nightmares were usually the same. I was visited by a king cobra that was bigger than me. I always tried to kill it, and it always tried to kill me. I had a sword. I would cut its head off, but it always grew back. I could not kill this snake, but when it bit me, it could do no harm. It just kept biting me, and it took me a while to realize it had no power to destroy me. Sometimes the dream involved a rattlesnake and it could do nothing but bite me. It could not cause any harm to me.

Once I realized that these snakes had no power to kill me, my life became better. My sleep improved. My mom thought there was some kind of spiritual warfare going on because of the way my dad was murdered. She thought that the cobra represented death. I know that it terrified the daylights out of me in the beginning. I was glad that I realized the snakes could not kill me or inflict any real pain. I tried to ignore the feelings and thoughts that the grief brought on. It did not work. I had no peace and I could not sleep. My diet was messed up. I had to work through the emotions.

One night, I went to a support group for people who had been victims of murder. I could not believe the amount of anger in that room. It was filled with vehement rage. It did not sit well with my soul. My mom felt the same way. One good thing came about from meeting as I met a man, and we talked for about an hour. He gave me some advice that stuck with me. He told me that his grief had cost him two marriages and a successful business. It even put his health at risk. The grief and anger literally bankrupted him. He told me to watch my anger and guard against it having control. He told me that the person who murdered his son had come close to murdering him too. He told me not to let that happen.

The Bible warns about anger and how it can be an opening for Satan to really trip a person up. I tried to ignore all of the above-mentioned feelings, but I could not. I had to seek help, and it came through a personal counselor and through the grief group. My mind was constantly flooded with insecurities, anger, sadness, and depression. Sometimes, they happened all at once. One minute, I could feel anger, and the next, I could feel sad. I was a mess, but it was okay.

What I was going through did not surprise God. After all, His Son was murdered as He hung upon the cross to take away the sin of the world. I found that the best thing to do was to spend time processing the grief. This did not mean that it had to be thought about twenty-four hours a day, seven days a week. We all need a break from our tragedies, and that is why it is good to have a close network of friends. Some of my friends proved to be worth more than gold.

I remember one of my best friends calling me and telling me some sort of lighthearted joke. Sometimes, I was not in the mood for it, but sometimes it helped me to get away from my own misery. Other times, there was no pulling me out. When going through grief, the heart can get so heavy that people need someone to help pull them away from the pain. I know it was hard to feel lighthearted, but sometimes it was a great solution and escape.

Looking Back While Going Forward

My dad and I were never very close. In fact, my dad was mentally and emotionally abusive to me. He made fun of my weight constantly and would often call me fat, dumb, and lazy. His words used to tear my heart apart. I had those tapes running through the recesses of my mind. I couldn't do anything right in his eyes as a kid or as a young adult.

I longed to hear my dad say that he loved me and was proud of me. That day did come. On that day, he told me how proud of me he was. He continued to tell me that he was proud of me for going to college and paying my own way in life. It was as if he had righted a lifetime of wrongs in that single moment of time. Never did my heart feel so much joy with my dad as it did then and when I repeated his words in my mind. I was so happy that I had that type of encounter with my father before he moved up north to work. I often clung to that conversation during great times of sorrow. It helped me and provided me with a lot of comfort as I went through the grief process. I know my other family members had some guilt about the way their relationships came to an end with my dad.

My mom took the murder extremely personal, even though she had nothing to do with it. The grief infiltrated our lives and really made us re-evaluate our own lives. I can remember my grief counselor suggesting that it was not good to make any major life-changing decisions for at least one year after a tragedy unless it was absolutely necessary.

I recommend finding a good grief group because it helps to share one's grief with others. It can also help a person find a new "normal." In the grief group, I found the depth I was looking for, and although no one else had suffered a loss caused by murder, I found the support to be extremely helpful.

I remember trying to focus on school. It was hard because I did not really care about anything anymore after I found out that my dad had been murdered. I thought that the best thing I could do was to succeed, which was exactly what I set my mind to do. However, my mind did not always cooperate. I had days where it was almost impossible to get out of bed, but I forced myself to continue on. Some days were easier than others, and then there were days where I could not win to save my life. I think what helped me to keep going was that I knew my mom wanted me to succeed, and after the final conversation with my dad, it would have been important to him as well. I still wanted to make something out of myself.

Emotional Challenges

As a guy, one of my strongest emotions was anger. When I first started the grief process, I had so much anger toward Fred who murdered my dad and God for allowing it to happen. It took quite a while for me to work through that anger. I also realized that I had certain triggers that would set me off. I remember my mom asking me to move some things into storage for her, and I lashed out and started throwing foul words into the air. I was almost uncontrollable. It wasn't until I calmed down and started to think about the situation rationally that I was able to see why that simple request evoked such a strong outburst.

I realized that my anger was because the last time I saw my dad, we were moving my mom's furniture into her apartment. I realized that helping someone move was a trigger for me. Another trigger was when my mom had car problems and she called me to fix them. That was a responsibility that belonged to my dad. Therefore, it evoked anger when my mom called on me to fix her car. Anger was my go-to emotion. I tried to maintain the status quo that society expected from me, but deep down, I was filled with anger, and I had a hard time letting it go.

Every now and then, I would totally break down, and the tears would roll almost uncontrollably. I hated to cry, but I loved the after-effects. It often resulted in peace of mind. Crying to me was much like working out at the gym. I never wanted to do it, but I always loved when it was done. It felt good and cleansing. I found out that crying was very healthy and cleansing in the grief process. Plus, crying is just a demonstration of the love that was felt for the person who passed.

There are so many emotions linked to the grief process. Sometimes I felt insecure, neurotic, angry, sad, exhausted, and guilty. I had a problem with being too hard on myself or expecting too much. This was where I relied on the grace of God.

I had a hard time with "The Cave Theory." I wanted to withdraw into my cave. When I was in there, no one could touch me or reach me. I isolated myself from my friends, family, and the world. It was not a productive way to deal with my problems, but it was extremely tempting because it felt safe. It usually made my problems worse.

I had my share of pity parties, but I don't think it ever helped. It was very self-defeating. I could put myself into a depression by feeling self-pity for myself.

Planning for the Holidays

Holidays were often a time of pain because this was a time that would have been spent with the loved one who was gone. I can remember days of grief for about a week leading up to a particular holiday. The grief group discussed ways to combat the sorrows that the holiday would bring. They also tried to help people come up with creative ideas on how a person might spend that day. When my family got together for the holidays, we usually felt sad at the beginning, but then my brother or I would usually stir things up and get people laughing.

I remember the first few holidays were just miserable. We tried to muscle through them. We didn't stop missing my dad, but we learned how to have a good time without his presence. Sometimes, we shared stories about him.

I remember one time, I got a camera as a Christmas present from work. I took the camera and started shooting the flash in the dog's eyes and in my dad's eyes. I kept finding a way to trick them both. The funny part was that after doing this a couple of times to the dog, she realized what I was doing and wouldn't let me trick her. My dad, on the other hand, kept falling for my tricks.

Neediness

I felt so helpless and needy. I also felt isolated and paralyzed emotionally, which made it hard for me to ask for help. I had to overcome my hang-ups to receive help. It would be nice to have people ask you how you are doing. However, that does not always take place. A person needs to be vulnerable and ask for help. People forget or they figure you have life all worked out. I don't think they do it to be mean, but they just don't understand that grief takes a lot longer to work through than a few weeks or a few months.

Paralysis and Isolation

During times of grief, paralysis and isolation are potentially two of the most dangerous emotions. Paralysis, for me, was not being able to perform everyday activities. I had a hard time going to school, work, or any other function for that matter. Grief had such a strong grip on my life that I did not want to continue on. It was important for me to identify this emotion when it came to visit. I tried to look at it as an emotion that was going to keep me down, and even though I had something so horrendous happen, I could not let the grief get the best of me.

I tried to contact someone when I was feeling this way. I often found myself contacting my mom. She could usually encourage me to go do the things that I needed to. Once I got out of the house, I generally felt better. I had encounters with people on occasions that would help. Someone would be friendly to me or start talking, which helped me to get out of my own thoughts.

Grief can be so intense that a person can easily lose sight of everyday life. I can remember being at the gym one day, thinking, *I'm just going to have a good day and not think about the sadness at all.* Toward the end of my workout, I was sitting on the lat-pull-down machine, and my tears just let loose. The sadness just overwhelmed me. I went outside and bawled my eyes out. It took me a while to realize that the grief needed to be dealt with as there was no escape from it.

I remember double-checking locks on the doors to make sure they were locked. Murder was a true violation. Nobody could steal anything more important to me than the life of a loved one.

Physical Exhaustion

My energy level was nowhere close to what it was before the grief process. I know that when I cried, it was as if I automatically turned on a sleeping switch. I got so tired when my emotions were being taxed. I did not have the same energy level that I had before everything happened. I have talked to numerous people, and they agreed that this was a very normal feeling. Everyone quickly forgot what I was going through. I'd like to think that people didn't mean to, but they just didn't understand.

I heard a lady in the grief group talking about her job at a local bank. She said that it had only been about three months since the passing of her mom. People told her to get over it. This was ridiculous. Who are people to tell someone to get over it? It was not something that one gets over. I can remember feeling like I was working through the grief, and then all of the sudden, it seemed like I was thrust right back to the beginning of the grief stages.

Learning to Face Emotions

I tried to learn to deal with my emotions in a positive manner. I wasn't successful 100 percent of the time. Sometimes, my emotions got me into trouble, and I paid a price for my poor decisions. I learned that it does no good to play games or to try and run and hide from the feelings. Grief must run its course. It is meant to change and shape you into a different person. It is meant to teach a lesson or lessons. It is often painful. I sometimes felt guilty for having a good time. I struggled with survivor's guilt.

Retail Therapy

I tried to combat my pain by buying things. I tried to escape the pain and feel good about life by buying clothes that I liked. Sometimes, this gave me a moment of happiness and something to talk about with friends and family. However, the happiness was fleeting. If I was lucky, the happiness would last for a few days, but I would still go shopping when, in reality, I needed to take care of my emotions. I remember shopping one time, and fifteen minutes later, I realized that the retail therapy was not working. I had emotions that needed to be dealt with. In truth, I could not really afford to keep participating in retail therapy. It usually left me with a void in my life that could not be replaced by material goods.

Hallucinations and Acceptance

I had to deal with hallucinations in my grief process. I don't mean hallucinations in the sense of drugs but in the sense of thinking that I was seeing a loved one while out in public.

I used to read meters for a public utility company, and I was walking down the street one day when I thought that I saw a gentleman down the street who looked like my dad. From a distance, the man appeared to be a spitting image of him. When I got closer, the man still appeared to be him, but when I walked right up next to the guy, I realized that it was not him. I was duped into believing he was. I wanted him to be. I wanted his death to be some elaborate hoax. My mind was trying to cope. I wanted this pain to subside and be a distant future. Luckily, I did not say anything to the gentleman to make a fool out of myself. I think this was a trick, a ruse, or a bad joke that my mind played on me. My mind played this trick on me a few more times. I so badly wanted it to be true. I wanted my dad back.

This was when the cold hard truth set in that *my dad was not coming back. He was gone.* I knew he was in heaven, but I wanted him to be here, even if he made my life harder. To make matters worse, I never had the opportunity to see my dad's body. We had to take the coroner at his word that my father was truly dead. My dad was cremated up north and then mailed down to my mom in a plastic lined box.

His body had been outside decaying from August to October. I have no doubt that it was my dad as the dental records matched, but I think it would've been easier to accept if I had been able to see his body.

I did see pictures of my dad from the photos that the Sonoma County Sheriff's Department had taken at the scene of the incident. They were gruesome. It was not a pretty sight. My father had been murdered while he was driving his van, and then, the man who did this threw my father out on the side of a mountain, hoping that my dad would never be found again. He wanted the body to go all of the way down into the King River that runs all of the way to the Pacific

Ocean. However, the man did not count on God being involved and knowing that we would need to have that information. It was a true miracle that my dad was found.

I had to come to the conclusion that *my dad was not coming back.* I wanted to wake up and find out that it was all some sort of secret ruse. My mind played tricks on me at night while I slept. I remember one night that I was sure that my dad was still alive. I held a conversation with my dad, and it seemed so real. I also remember telling my dad in the dream that he could not still be alive. I was worried that my mom was going to have to repay the little bit of life insurance money that she had received.

Many times, I had nightmares where people were chasing me and trying to kill me. It was such an awful feeling, but after talking to a psychologist, I came to the realization that what I was facing was fear because of what happened to my dad. I tried to write down my nightmares when I remembered them. I also talked about them. They did subside as time went on and as I worked through the thoughts.

Some dreams were comforting. I remember one night when I was asleep, I heard my father's voice, and he told me that he was fine and in heaven. This provided me with great comfort. I heard his voice almost audibly. It was kind of hard to explain, but I truly believe that it was him and that God allowed him to speak to me for a moment. I told my mom about this. She told me that she also had a similar encounter with my dad one night. The reason she knows it was him is because he called her by a nickname that only the two of them knew. He told her that he was fine. We were both comforted by talking about this scenario.

I wish you well on your journey though the valley of grief. I pray that God will fill your hearts and heal you from the loss that you have experienced. In the precious name of Jesus. Amen!

About the Author

Jack Brant Jr. holds a master of theology degree from Talbot School of Theology and a bachelor of arts degree in English from California State University of Fullerton. He facilitated for many years in the grief group at First Evangelical Free Church of Fullerton and continues to be of service at his current church. He lived in Southern California for over thirty years when he decided it was time to move to South Carolina with his wife, Jenny.

CPSIA information can be obtained
at www.ICGtesting.com
Printed in the USA
FSHW012104190221
78779FS